B-17 FLYING FORTRESS
A Bombing Legend

MICHAEL O'LEARY

OSPREY
AEROSPACE

Published in 1992 by
Osprey Publishing Limited
Michelin House, 81 Fulham Road, London, SW3 6RB
Reprinted Spring 1994

British Library Cataloguing in Publication Data

ISBN 1 85532 197 1

Editor Tony Holmes
Page design by Paul Kime
Printed in Hong Kong

Front cover Easing ever closer to the author's camera-ship, B-17G *Miss Museum of Flying* gleams in the California sun. The standards achieved by the restoration team during the rebuild of this 'metal monster' stand out for all to see. Only the chin turret, devoid of its twin 0.50 inch Browning guns, is lacking its true wartime appearance, this minor discrepancy being corrected when the bomber was sent to Fort Lauderdale, Florida, in June 1991 for further restoration

Back cover Scantily clad women and B-17 noses were meant for each other, and the Confederate Air Force's Flying Fortress doesn't disappoint! The rugged construction of the veteran bomber is beautifully picked out in the warm light, the mass of rivets and shaped aluminium giving the B-17 an air of impregnability

Title page The distinctive nose shape of the B-17G is known worldwide. The chin turret was added as a deterrent to head-on attacks by *Luftwaffe* fighters as the bombers battled their way into Germany. *Texas Raiders* is one of two B-17s operated by the Confederate Air Force, and its interior has been outfitted with much original military gear

For a catalogue of all books published by Osprey Aerospace
please write to:

**The Marketing Department, Octopus Illustrated Books,
1st Floor, Michelin House, 81 Fulham Road, London SW3 6RB**

Few aircraft are more graceful in the air than the Flying Fortress, as proven here by *Miss Museum of Flying*, seen over a fog deck near Santa Maria, California

Introduction

While preparing this book, I tried to recall the first time I saw a B-17. Looking back, I believe it was at Bunker Hill AFB (now Grissom AFB) in Peru, Indiana. The old 'Fort was being used as a gate guardian and was not in the best of shape, having been picked at by souvenir hunters over the years. This was in the early 1960s and the base also had a Consolidated PB4Y Privateer that had landed with an engine out and stayed. The Navy didn't want it back and the base fire section eventually burned the aircraft. The B-17G survived and is now part of a small USAF heritage museum at the field. It's still in terrible shape!

One of the few efficient actions undertaken by the American government was the mass scrapping of the aircraft that had won World War 2. Photographs taken at Kingman, Arizona, and other similar depots in 1946 show hundreds if not thousands of bombers and fighters awaiting their turn at the smelter. The military and government saw little if any need to preserve examples for future generations, and it was left to a handful of civilians to purchase a few B-17s that would go on to lead hard working lives hauling cargo, spraying bugs, and fighting forest fires.

During the 1970s, some of these old workhorses began to retire, being traded in for newer equipment to the USAF Museum, who then allocated the aircraft to various bases where they would never fly again. Fortunately, the aircraft you see flying on these pages are the result of lots of hard work on the part of individuals and museums who are keeping the Flying Fortress where it belongs—in the air. Thanks to all the people involved for making their aircraft available for photography and to William T Larkins, James Farmer and Scott Thompson for their pioneering research into the history of the surviving B-17s. Thanks is also due to Bruce Guberman who served as camera plane pilot for the majority of the aerial photography.

Michael O'Leary pictured below is the associate publisher of a group of aeronautical magazines. This is his seventh book for Osprey.

Right Operating four-engined piston bombers in the 1990s is a more and more difficult proposition. Even the availability of avgas is questionable in the future as requirements for the fuel decrease and demands from environmentalists increase. The 100LL being pumped into the 'Fort is a far cry from the octane rich fuels of World War 2

Contents

Workhorse of the sky

Right In October 1985, Globe Air decided to auction off its remaining fleet of Flying Fortresses and other veteran World War 2 air attack and agricultural aircraft. Photographed shortly before the auction, the 'Forts stand silent as they await new owners. Fortunately, all four B-17s involved in the auction have found new homes that are restoring the aircraft back to pristine condition

Below For many years, the B-17 was the mainstay of the 'heavy' portion of America's air attack (fire bombing) fleet. However, age and newer equipment caused all the 'Forts to be retired by 1985. Unfortunately, many flying aircraft were traded for newer equipment to the USAF Museum programme, and once-proud flying B-17s are now static gate guards at various USAF bases

Above B-17G USAAF s/n 44-85806 N117W was one of the first Flying Fortresses converted for aerial spraying and was operated by the Biegert brothers in Phoenix, Arizona, along with sister-ship B-17F N17W. As can be seen, the aircraft was fitted with underwing spray bars and huge surplus drop tanks. In December 1964, the 'Fort was sold to Bolivian Air System in La Paz, but did not last long, being written off on 16 December of the same year!

Right The hulk of B-17G-75-DL USAAF s/n 44-83316 at Chino, California, on 30 July 1967 when it was being utilized as a prop for the television series *Twelve O'Clock High*. Delivered to the USAAF on 17 February 1945, the aircraft appears to have been flown to Britain shortly afterwards and may have gone into storage. At the end of the war in Europe, the 'Fort was assigned to Air Forces Europe and flew out of Rhein Main, eventually being modified to a VB-17G. During the late 1940s and early 1950s, the craft flew with several units in Germany before flying back to Fairfax AFB, Virginia, in late 1952, and continued to operate until being put into storage in 1956. Removed from storage in 1959, the 'Fort flew to Norton AFB in California as part of a proposed aviation museum. However, a new base commander was unsympathetic to the project and the aircraft was partially scrapped before the fuselage was moved to Chino for television use. During this time, portions were burned, hacked at, and otherwise heavily damaged. However, the hulk was purchased by Black Hills Aviation, and hauled to Spearfish, South Dakota. The nose of '316 was used to rebuild N6694C which had been used as a five-engine test bed by Curtiss-Wright. What was left of '316 kept moving and is now owned by Kermit Weeks, who may use the parts in a projected B-17 rebuild

Photographed by the late Stephen Piercey (the ultimate propliner buff) in Bolivia during November 1977, this rare B-17E, USAAF s/n 41-9210 CP-753, was being operated as a meat hauler by *Frigerificos Reyes* and was in typically worn condition. Eventually abandoned engineless and forgotten at La Paz, the aircraft was rescued by Don Whittington in 1990 and flown back to his base at Fort Lauderdale (as N17WJ), where it is now being restored to mint condition, a task which includes reskinning most of the airframe

B-17G-105-VE USAAF s/n 44-85738 during its long slide to oblivion at Tulare, California, during June 1967. Parked alongside Highway 99, the aircraft has been the subject of vandals, poor weather and a nearly destructive truck accident. Thought to be the last survivor of *Operation Crossroads*—the atomic bomb testing in the South Pacific—the aircraft was delivered on 18 May 1945 and then went into storage, eventually being withdrawn for the *Crossroads* mission and modified as a DB-17G drone director. The tests took place at Bikini Atoll and involved the destruction of over 100 warships. The drone director would 'fly' drone B-17s through the radioactive areas to sample the air. Brought back to the US in mid-1946, the aircraft was transferred to different units as a drone director and in 1958 '738 was selected for preservation. Tulare took the aircraft because General Maurice Preston, World War 2 commander of the 379th Bomb Group, had been born in the town. Accordingly, the aircraft was transferred and located at the crop duster airport, the USAF even supplying a set of power turrets. The airframe quickly deteriorated and in 1971 was towed by a tractor to a restaurant where it could be better protected. Once the USAF found the aircraft to be on private property, they demanded it be towed back to the airport, which was done in 1981. In August 1982, an out-of-control semi crashed into the bomber, shoving it 30 feet and heavily damaging the tail section. A number of reputable groups have tried to save the weary bomber but the USAF Museum refuses to let it go and the aircraft remains a gutted eyesore

PB-1W BuNo 77227 N5226V, ex-VW-2, is typical of what the Navy aircraft looked like after being removed from storage. N5226V was photographed during March 1962. At this point, N5226V was still fitted with the large belly radome and ADF 'football' on the nose. Sold to *Compania Boliviana de Rutas Aereas* in 1964, the PB-1W (ex-USAAF s/n 44-83858) was destroyed in a crash at Santa Ana, Bolivia, on 21 February 1965

As previously noted, Curtiss-Wright obtained B-17G USAAF s/n 44-85813 for conversion to a five-engined test bed, mounting a R-3350 turbo-compound radial in the nose. Given the civil registration N6694C, the B-17 was obtained by Black Hills Aviation, who had to undertake the daunting task of rebuilding the forward fuselage as the cockpit had been relocated several feet to the rear to accommodate the engine. Once work was finished, Black Hills began operating the very austere 'Fort as Tanker 12C, seen during August 1973 at Omak, Washington. The bomber crashed on take-off at Bear Pen, North Carolina, soon after. However, the remains have been purchased by Tom Reilly in Florida and will be used with the surviving parts of the only other five-engined 'Fort to eventually create a stock B-17G

Once denuded of its radar belly pod and interior radar screens, PB-1W N5226V was fitted with a borate tank in the bomb bay and spray bars under the wings to take care of both of the basic missions for which the 'Fort was utilized during the 1960s. Seen at Long Beach, California, on 11 November 1962, N5226V wears the colours of 'C' Air, who also operated a wide variety of ex-military aircraft as can be seen from the line-up behind the 'Fort, including Avengers, a Mitchell, a Harpoon and a Catalina

Right One of the most intriguing civil Fortresses is N809Z, seen at Marana, Arizona, on 22 March 1966. B-17 historian Scott Thompson has discovered that the true USAAF s/n is apparently 44-85531 rather than 44-83785 as listed by the FAA. The reason for the confusion? It appears that the aircraft was extensively utilized by the Central Intelligence Agency during the 1950s and 1960s for a variety of covert operations. When photographed, the B-17 was being operated by Intermountain Aviation, this company acting as a front operation for the CIA, and Marana Air Park, then a remote desert location between Tucson and Phoenix, was an ideal place to carry out operations that were unorthodox in nature. As can be seen, the aircraft was fitted with a padded open exit in the tail gun position and a huge set of 'pinchers' in the nose, which were apparently used to snatch agents that were lifted by helium balloons. Oddly, the aircraft was utilized in the James Bond film *Thunderball*. The B-17 was converted to Tanker 22 in 1969 was but not overly utilized. When its cover was exposed during the 1970s, Intermountain went out of business and the ownership of the aircraft was obtained by Evergreen Helicopters in 1975, who changed the registration to N207EV in 1979. Evergreen took over most of Marana (now named Pinal Airpark to disassociate it from its CIA past). In the late 1980s, a restoration project began to bring the 'Fort back to military configuration and it is now in the colours of the 490th Bomb Group, Eighth Air Force

Above The last air force to operate the 'Fort was Brazil's, and B-17G-90-DL USAAF s/n 44-83663 BAF5400 N47780 is seen shortly after arrival in the United States during October 1968 as a gift for the USAF Museum. The BAF operated a dozen 'Forts over the years. The USAF placed the aircraft in storage and in 1973 worked a deal with Dave Tallichet who got the B-17 airworthy and ferried it to Chino

PB-1G BuNo 77255 (USAAF s/n 44-85829) N3193G flew its last mission with the US Coast Guard during October 1959. The aircraft was then sold at auction from CGAS Elizabeth City, North Carolina, to Ace Smelting for $5887.93. Shortly afterwards, the plane was ferried to Phoenix and then sold to Fairchild Aerial Survey. The interior was reworked to accommodate survey equipment and the position occupied by the ball turret was fitted with a large camera. Painted in Fairchild's distinctive house colours of orange, blue and white, the aircraft was operated by the company for five years. Ownership eventually passed to the Biegert brothers who, as they had done with other 'Forts, fitted the aircraft as a sprayer. By 1966, the 'Fort had become the property of Aircraft Specialities, who modified the B-17 for firebombing. The aircraft flew to Hawaii in 1969 for the filming of *Tora! Tora! Tora!*, and then returned for continued firebombing. After the 1985 Globe Air auction, the bomber passed to the Yankee Air Force, Ypsilanti, Michigan, who are carrying out a complete rebuild back to stock condition

Above The battered remains of B-17G-95-DL USAAF s/n 44-83722 are seen at Falcon Field during 1968. This is one of two atom bomb test aircraft acquired by Aviation Specialities. This particular aircraft had been modified to TB-17H configuration with a Higgins life boat and search radar. It was transferred to Yucca Flats and very heavily damaged during several above ground atomic bomb tests. Hauled to Falcon Field in May 1965, the aircraft provided parts for the company's fleet of 'Forts. In October 1985, the hulk was purchased by collector Kermit Weeks and is stored in the California desert

Above left At Chino in November 1975, the aircraft had a dull coat of aluminum sprayed over its attractive Brazilian AF markings. In 1977, the bomber was flown to Topeka where it remained until 1980 when it was flown to St Petersburg, Florida, and painted in Olive Drab camouflage. The condition of the aircraft went downhill rapidly from that point on. The USAF finally took it back in 1983 and had it disassembled and fitted into a C-5A for the journey to Hill AFB, Utah, where it is on display today

Left B-17G USAAF s/n 42-102715 N66573 was, as can be seen by the distinctive colours, operated by Fairchild Aerial Surveys from 1953 to 1961 when it was sold as an aerial tanker to Ewing Aviation and later to Black Hills Aviation. Because of its scallop paint design, the aircraft was dubbed the 'batmobile'. Flying as Tanker 10, the aircraft crashed on a firebombing mission at Cayuse Saddle, Montana, during 1979

Shoo Shoo Shoo Baby

Unlike the Royal Air Force, the USAF does not, unfortunately, maintain any form of memorial flight, nor does it have any desire to do so. This is doubly unfortunate since the most in-depth restoration of a Flying Fortress took place on B-17G-35-BO s/n 42-32076, which made only a few flights before being ensconced in the USAF Museum. In 1972, the *Institut Geographique National* (IGN) donated the hulk of F-BGSH to the museum since the aircraft was the only known surviving combat veteran 'Fort, having flown with the 91st Bomb Group out of Bassingbourn, that could possibly be returned to flying condition. The aircraft was moved from France by C-5A Galaxy, and the 512th Military Airlift Wing, Dover AFB, volunteered to take on the daunting task, with restoration commencing in 1978. As can be seen in Budd Davisson's magnificent photograph, the hard work of the volunteers created one of the most splendid B-17 restorations ever completed

Left The crew chief named the B-17 *Shoo Shoo Baby*, after a song popular in 1943, and, the extra *Shoo* was added a bit later. Usually each bomb group had an artist and *Baby* received an attractive pin-up courtesy of Sgt Tony Starcer. Years later, a now-retired Starcer travelled to Dover to recreate his art work on the bomber. Unfortunately, Starcer passed away before the bomber flew once again. On 29 May 1944, *'Baby* was on a mission to Pozan, Poland, to bomb a Focke-Wulf factory. While over Germany, an engine lost oil pressure and the crew attempted to feather the prop, but for some reason it refused to freewheel in the slipstream and the drag increased accordingly. Keeping with the formation for self-defence, *'Baby* did drop its bombs on the assigned target. However, a second engine was damaged by flak and the B-17 dropped out of formation. Lt Robert Guenther set course for neutral Sweden while the crew jettisoned everything that was not riveted down to help reduce weight and maintain altitude

Above The descending *'Baby* was picked up by Swedish fighters and guided to the field at Malmo, and whilst on finals, a third engine quit. On the field, the crew was interned by Swedish soldiers and the B-17 joined the many other USAAF aircraft already on hand. In late 1944, the crew was handed over to the American authorities in exchange for the Swedish government receiving nine B-17s for $1 each. The Swedes wanted to convert the aircraft into civil airliners and *'Baby* was so modified, emerging with an elongated nose, airline interior, extra windows and seating for 14 passengers. Registered SE-BAP, the aircraft was sold to Denmark as an airliner but eventually entered Danish military service, operating until late 1953 when withdrawn from service. In 1955, the aircraft was purchased by the *IGN* and flown to France for further modification as an aerial mapping platform

IGN registered *Baby* as F-BGSH and flew it until mid-1961 when it was withdrawn from service and stripped of useful parts and abandoned. Fortunately, the aircraft was eventually transferred to the USAF Museum, but in the loading process the wing centre section was allegedly ruined by USAF personnel who cut the aircraft apart to get it into the C-5A. Once at Dover AFB, the amount of work that went into the bomber was truly awe-inspiring as the volunteers wanted to make the aircraft as authentic as possible, collecting original bits of interior from around the globe. The many civilian modifications had to be removed and a repairable centre section was obtained. Engines and props were overhauled and much reskinning was undertaken under the supervision of project director Ray McCloskey, and a core team of six men, who worked over nine years to insure a flawless first flight in August 1988 with Bill 'Doc' Hospers doing the piloting honours. On 13 October, several short hops were made at the base and the plane was then flown to enshrinement at the USAF Museum, never to fly again

November Seventeen Whiskey

Out to pasture. Operated by Globe Air during the closing days of its aerial attack life, B-17F-70-BO USAAF s/n 42-29782 N17W sits on the ramp at Falcon Field, Mesa, Arizona, in preparation for the October 1985 auction that would see Globe sell off its fleet of aircraft and parts in what would become the last great warbird auction. One of the longest survivors of the civil 'Fort population, the aircraft was delivered by Boeing to the USAAF on 13 February 1943, and flown to the Cheyenne, Wyoming, modification centre that was being efficiently run by United Airlines for the fitting of the latest combat and equipment updates

Left Parked amongst other 'Forts at Mesa on 20 February 1972, N17W has a decidedly tired appearance, perhaps due to its constant operation for, at that time, nearly 30 years. After visiting the mod centre, '782 was assigned to a training unit in California to instruct pilots and crews. From there the aircraft went through a military overhaul and another training assignment in Washington. The loss of a main gear tyre on 20 September 1943 resulted in damage to the right wing and its engines and propellers. This was repaired and the aircraft continued on

Above There is some indication that '782 went 'overseas' during early 1944 but it is doubtful the aircraft would have been sent to a combat unit since newer and better aircraft were available. However, it is known that the B-17F went to Drew Field, Montana, during May 1944 to continue in the training mission and stayed there until sent to the big surplus lot in Altus, Oklahoma, for scrapping or disposal. The photograph illustrates N17W at Phoenix during December 1960 when it was being operated as a very basic firebomber by the Biegert Brothers, who had obtained the aircraft through a lengthy and costly process

Right Wearing its *Memphis Belle* warpaint, N17W is seen undergoing an engine test at Geneseo, New York, during August 1990. After the cessation of hostilities the B-17F was offered for free as a 'war memorial' to any town that was interested and the 'Fort was transferred to Stuttgart, Arkansas, for display on 10 September 1947, remaining the property of the Federal Government, a fact that was quickly forgotten

Below N17W makes a run past the cameras during the filming of *Memphis Belle* as one of two 'Forts flown to Britain from America to take part in the 1990 filming. The Biegerts converted N17W as a sprayer and installed seven tanks in the aircraft, including two giant 450-gallon droptanks off an F-94 under the wing (giving the aircraft an imposing 3100 gallon spraying capacity), and immediately began working the 'Fort across the country. In late 1961, it was sold to Abe Sellards who converted N17W into a pure aerial tanker, the aircraft merging into the growing B-17 fleet operated by Aviation Specialities. Flying as Tanker 84 and 04, the aircraft operated around the country, but found time to appear in *Tora! Tora! Tora!* and *1000 Plane Raid*. In the October 1985 auction, the bomber was sold to Seattle businessman Robert Richardson. Richardson was a member of the Museum of Flight in Seattle and had thoughts about donating the aircraft to the museum (*Warner Bros.*)

Above Already looking worse for wear when flown to Stuttgart, the B-17F rapidly slid downhill. The majority of its military equipment, including all turrets, had already been removed and the sturdy citizens of Stuttgart quickly tired of their 'eyesore'. A local citizen illegally purchased the bomber from the stalwart city council and quickly sold the aircraft to Max and John Biegert in mid-1953. However, the government quickly caught on to this. With the registration N17W crudely affixed to its side, the B-17F prepares to depart Geneseo for Boeing Field in Seattle during 1990. The Biegert brothers had taken the aircraft apart and moved it to the local airport for reassembly and return to flying condition when the Feds intervened and refused to issue a permit to fly. However, a compromise was reached when the Biegerts paid the Feds a whopping $20,000 for the aircraft—surely the highest price paid for a surplus 'Fort!

Right Are N17W's Wrights to remain forever still? In July 1989, N17W was flown to Britain to participate in the making of *Memphis Belle*. During this time Richardson became closely associated with the National Warplane Museum in Geneseo, and he began to give serious thought about selling N17W to this organization. However, in 1990 Richardson died suddenly and his will honoured the transfer of the B-17 to Seattle. The bomber was made airworthy at Geneseo and flown cross-country to Washington State, performing perhaps its last flight in the process as the museum wants to hang it inside its main building

Memphis Belle

The 1990 release of *Memphis Belle* from Warner Bros introduced a whole new generation to the Flying Fortress. Filmed in Britain, the production utilized Mustangs, Spanish-built Hispano *Buchons*, and five B-17s, two of which were flown from the United States to participate. One of the two was B-17G-85-DL USAAF 44-83546 N3703G, which belongs to the Military Aircraft Restoration Corporation. Dave Tallichet is seen flying the aircraft over Geneseo, New York, after bringing the B-17 back from Britain during August 1989. The well-weathered appearance of the film paint is clearly visible

By 16 August 1991, N3703G was back in full *Memphis Belle* colours, the conversion resulting in a fairly authentic looking B-17F, seen here being flown by Tallichet over Geneseo. The annual August National Warbird Museum (NWM) airshow has been the yearly gathering point for the surviving B-17 population. This aircraft was built at the Douglas Long Beach factory and delivered to the military on 3 April 1945. Like many other late build 'Forts, the aircraft was sent to a modification depot and then into storage at Patterson Field, Ohio. When required, the aircraft was pulled from storage and converted into a CB-17G staff transport

Right Photographed during August 1985, Tallichet cruises over Madera, California, during that town's annual warbird airshow. As can be seen, at this point in time, the B-17 differed in a number of ways from its *Memphis Belle* configuration. During its military service, the aircraft was assigned to many stateside bases before heading off to Weisbaden, Germany, to service the 501st Strategic Reconnaissance Group and eventually became the personal aircraft of General Idwall Edwards, commander Air Forces Europe. The aircraft was redesignated VB-17G on 16 October 1948 and then returned to the 'States for service at Andrews and Offut AFBs

Below Seen during *Memphis Belle* filming, N3703G made a particularly good representation of a combat-weary B-17F with its various layers of movie paint and artificial weathering. After the start of the Korean War, '546 made the long flight to Japan where it operated from Haneda. A trip was made back to the USA for overhaul in 1952, followed by a return to Japan. In 1954, the 'Fort was assigned to Davis-Monthan AFB for indefinite storage *(Warner Bros.)*

Above In this scene from the film, some of the actors relax while N3703G forms an imposing background. During the filming of *Memphis Belle*, the bomber carried a number of other identities including *Lady Jane, Gee Whiz, Baby Ruth, Windy City* and *My Zita*, along with a number of differing code letters. In 1959, the USAF decided to dispose of the majority of its stored 'Forts and '546 went for a modest $2686.86 to the National Metals Company in Phoenix who, judging by the name, must have been a scrap metal merchant (*Warner Bros.*)

Right The assembled group of actors that comprised the crew of the *Memphis Belle* are seen in front of 'their' aircraft. Fortunately, National Metals sold '546 rather than scrapping it, the weary bomber going to Fastway Air in Long Beach, the airport at where it was originally built. Fastway registered their 'Fort as N3703G and painted the aircraft in a very attractive blue and white scheme. They had plans to work the bomber for fire-fighting and installed two 900 gallon fire retardant tanks, along with associated plumbing, and '03G became one of the first 'Forts used as a firebomber. At this time, Fastway Air also owned N3702G and both B-17s became familiar sights at air attack bases around the country (*Warner Bros.*)

Above N3703G at Porterville, California, during September 1974 when it was being operated as tanker 78E by TBM Inc. Most of the civilian Flying Fortresses were operated as aerial tankers and this hazardous occupation claimed a number of aircraft and crews. However, if it had not been for the fire fighting mission, very few 'Forts would survive today

Left In between attending many airshows across the country, N3703G spends a considerable amount of time at Chino, which is home base for the Military Aircraft Restoration Corporation. This photo illustrates the nose art as well as the matching painted A-2 jacket in the bombardier's compartment. In 1967, Fastway's two 'Forts were purchased by TBM Incorporated, who continued to utilize the aircraft in the firebombing role. As the 'Forts got older and newer aircraft became available, '02G was traded to the USAF Museum—an unfortunate fate since many flyable B-17s are now static 'gate guards' at various USAF bases. A better fate awaited N3703G and the aircraft was purchased by David Tallichet, who flew B-17s during World War 2, and in 1986 it was converted back to military configuration. A Sperry top turret from a wrecked South Pacific B-17 was added along with a Cheyenne tail turret. An operational ball turret is fitted and the bomb bay doors work

Fuddy Duddy

Right The small, historic village of Geneseo, in upstate New York, is home to a thriving, albeit unlikely for the location, organization known as the National Warplane Museum. Created by Austin Wadsworth and several other local aviation enthusiasts in the early 1980s, the NWM is now a nationally-recognized aviation museum that honours the American aviation effort during World War 2 and Korea. One of the real stars of the museum's expanding collection of warbirds is Boeing B-17G-85-DL (Douglas-built) USAAF 44-83563 N9563Z, which is seen in this August 1989 view low over the scenic countryside near its home base. Note the early-style upper turret and lack of the distinguishing chin turret

Below N9563Z has not been a warbird content to rest on its laurels as the Flying Fortress has led an active life since the day it was built. Accepted from the Long Beach, California, factory on 7 April 1945, the B-17 was flown to storage at Patterson Field, Ohio, where it resided for just a month before being modified as a CB-17G staff transport and flown to the Philippines. The aircraft would go on to lead a ten-year service life as a VIP transport. This photograph, taken on 16 August 1991, shows the latest configuration of *Fuddy Duddy* with its new (replica) chin turret installed along with the cheek nose gun positions and various other small refinements which are part of the NWM's long-term goal to return the aircraft to original wartime configuration

Fuddy Duddy turns final for Geneseo's famed 'cornfield' runway with power back and flaps down during August 1990. By this time, the inaccurate (for a G-model) top turret had 'exploded', its aged plexiglass giving way to the pressure of airspeed. An accurate turret is currently being built. In 1947, this aircraft was assigned to the Far East Air Force's Pacific Air Services Command and became a VB-17G, going on to see service in Japan during the Korean War with the 3rd Bomb Wing, which was operating Douglas A-26 Invaders at the time and used the 'Fort as a hack

Above Up close and personal. This August 1991 view illustrates some of the detail work undertaken by the NWM, including waist gun positions (with canvas covers around the swivel mounts for the .50 calibre Brownings) and the ball turret—all turrets for the 'Fort have become collector's items and are very hard to find, as well as being extremely pricey. In 1952, '563 flew back to Olmsted AFB, Pennsylvania, for an overhaul and then back to Japan (avgas was cheap then) to continue VIP hauling duties with the 6000th Base Service Group, where the aircraft remained until June 1955

Left Just holding above Geneseo's corn field runway, N9563Z prepares to touch down during August 1990 while a pair of military-marked Ercoupes (yes, the USAAC did have a few YO-53As!) prepare to take-off. The aircraft is finished in the markings of *Fuddy Duddy*, a B-17G operated by the 447th Bomb Group from Rattlesdan, England

In about the most plain markings possible, N9563Z taxies across the grass at Mt Hope Airfield, Hamilton, Ontario, Canada, during June 1986—shortly after the acquisition of the 'Fort by the NWM. After being retired from USAF service, the aircraft was flown from Haneda to Davis-Monthan AFB in Arizona to join the very few surviving B-17s left in storage. The aircraft remained tied to the desert floor until 18 August 1959, when it was sold surplus for $3156 to American Compressed Steel Corporation of Cincinnati, Ohio

High over Hamilton, N9563Z displays the B-17G's distinctive profile. On 9 May 1960, the aircraft became the property of Aero-American Corporation, which was apparently a branch of American Compressed Steel, and several researchers have linked the companies as operating arms of the CIA, who used them to move World War 2 aircraft to various hot spots around the globe. Located at the then-remote Ryan Field near Tucson, Gregory Board and his Aero-American employees got '563 and two other 'Forts airworthy and ferried the aircraft to Ryan. In late 1960, all three B-17s went to Brownsville, Texas, where they had large cargo doors installed on the right rear fuselage and, in this photo, the door is made evident by the patch of shiny aluminum. Two of the modified B-17s were sold off but N9563Z sat at Ryan, awaiting an interested buyer

The interested buyer for N9563Z came in an odd form: Columbia Pictures of Hollywood. British pilot John Crewdson (head of Film Aviation Service Ltd) had been contracted to find three B-17s to be used in the filming of John Hersey's novel *The War Lover*. N9563Z was quickly purchased—Crewdson had just missed out on three Israeli 'Forts that had been scrapped, although he was able to purchase one fuselage for interior scene filming. Board and his crew managed to scrounge turrets and some other military equipment to get the aircraft to look like an operational wartime bomber. The B-17 is seen after its return from filming in Britain at Tucson during 28 December 1962 with *The War Lover* boldly emblazoned under the wing. When the film opened in major cities, the B-17 would fly over and 'bomb' the town with leaflets to promote the motion picture, which starred Steve McQueen and Robert Wagner. Anyone who is interested in B-17s should try to find a copy of Martin Caidin's *Everything but the Flak*, which details the flight of N9563Z and two other B-17s across the Atlantic to the film location in Britain. Caidin flew as co-pilot and recounts the tale in great colour. Unfortunately, after completion of filming the other two B-17s were left in Britain and quickly scrapped (an almost unthinkable act by today's standards and values). N9563Z headed back home for the promotional mission and an entirely new career

Above Detail of N9563Z's nose shows the markings for the promotion tour, along with the rather beaten up chin turret which is minus its customary fairing

Above right Once the film was released, Columbia had very little interest in the continued ownership of a World War 2 bomber, and N9563Z was sold on 23 February 1963 to nearby Aviation Specialities at Falcon Field, Mesa, Arizona. The company was in the firebombing and crop spraying business and as soon as '63Z arrived at Falcon Field, all military gear was stripped out and a borate tank and associated equipment was installed in the bomb bay, the 'Fort soon going back to work fighting a new and deadly enemy in one of the most hazardous of aviation careers. In this view, N9563Z is seen at Falcon Field during April 1968 under the guise of Tanker 24E

Right N9563Z served the company faithfully in its firebombing role, but took some time off to appear in another film epic. Aircraft Specialities (the company had received a new name) was contracted to provide five B-17s for the film *Tora! Tora! Tora!* Painted in period markings with turrets back in place, the five B-17s staged out of Oakland, California, and headed for Hawaii during 1968. The filming was successful and the planes returned to their firebombing work. In 1981, the company once again reorganized, this time as Globe Air, and continued their operations with a wide variety of surplus aircraft. In 1985, the partners decided to liquidate their assets and a huge auction was held during October 1985, which saw N9563Z sold in flying condition to the NWM for what was then the princely sum of $250,000

Sentimental Journey

Possibly the most famous of all surviving Flying Fortresses is B-17G-85-DL (USAAF s/n 44-83514) N9323Z, which is operated by the Confederate Air Force's Arizona Wing as *Sentimental Journey*. The reason for the fame is simple since the CAF campaigns the aircraft across the country to airshows and displays, and more people have toured this vintage bomber than any other 'Fort. The late afternoon sun shows off the bomber's gleaming skin to advantage as the 'Fort flies over a field near Geneseo, New York, on 16 August 1991. The aircraft was delivered to the USAAF from the Douglas factory in Long Beach during March 1945, but its early military history is obscure since many of the necessary records are not in the military's files

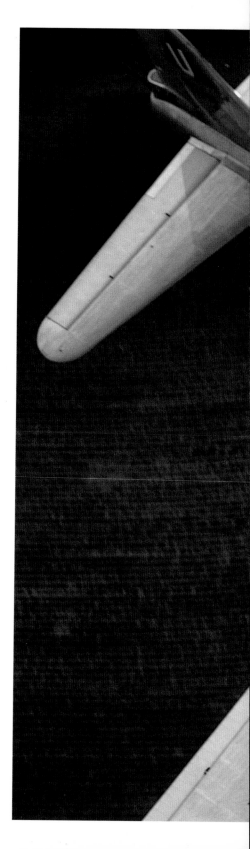

Right With Dick Churchill in the left seat, *Sentimental Journey* makes an impressive sight as it tracks through the sky. One of the most authentically furnished of all surviving B-17s, the aircraft is extremely popular with airshow spectators. During its military service, '514 probably went into storage after being delivered and passing through one of the modification facilities. It is thought that the aircraft may have served in the Far East, after being pulled from storage and eventually finding its way to the 3250th Drone Group, based at Eglin AFB in Florida, some time around 1954–55

Overleaf Dick Churchill joins up with the CAF's other 'Fort, *Texas Raiders*, for a family portrait on 15 August 1991. The natural metal finish of and the weathered Olive Drab and Neutral Grey camouflage on the two aircraft are very representative of the bomber formations that were heading to Germany in late 1944 and early 1945. The military records for '514 do not surface until 1956 and at that late date the aircraft was with the 3215th Drone Squadron, Patrick AFB, Florida, as a DB-17P drone director

Above Great restorations do not usually happen in a short period of time, unless the owner is extremely wealthy and money is little or no object. *Sentimental Journey* has been a progressive flying restoration, with original military bits and pieces added as time and money permit. Photographed on 7 December 1986, N9323Z begins to descend to make a pass over a group of veterans commemorating the anniversary of Pearl Harbor in Burbank, California. The 'Fort is ably escorted by the late, great Dave Zeuschel flying one of Joe Kasparoff's stable of Mustangs. When put up for surplus, '514 was purchased by Acme Aircraft Parts in lovely downtown Compton, California, for $5289.99 on 31 July 1959. Acme had the aircraft licensed but probably did little work on it before selling it to Western Air Industries, Anderson, California, in late 1960 for $8000

Left N9323Z rumbles over the yearly gathering point for 'Forts—Geneseo, New York, during the annual 1991 airshow. The aircraft remained in the Florida area as a DB-17P for the balance of its military career, before flying to Davis-Monthan AFB in 1959 for storage as one of the USAF's last 'Forts. Since 1959 was the year for selling off the USAF's remaining B-17 inventory, '514's life in storage was very brief

Above *Sentimental Journey* is seen against a hazy Geneseo background as the 'Fort prepares to make a pass over the runway in August 1991. Western Air had purchased N9323Z for conversion to an aerial tanker and this was undertaken at their base when two 1000 gallon tanks and associated equipment was installed. At this time, the majority of the original military equipment was removed and tossed aside, being deemed of little value

Right Gear down but flaps still up, N9323Z turns base leg for finals to the Madera Airport in central California during that town's annual warbird airshow in August 1982. Assigned the distinctive identification of Tanker 17 with Western Air, the aircraft went to work fighting major conflagrations across the United States

Left One of N9323Z's Wrights belches to life amongst a gathering of CAF heavy iron including the Boeing B-29 Superfortress and Consolidated LB-30 Liberator during the annual May 1988 Planes of Fame Airshow at Chino, California, which, unfortunately, is no longer held

Above A very unfortunate accident occurred to *Sentimental Journey* during November 1988 when a brake failure caused the aircraft to veer off the Burbank Airport runway, smash into a dumpster and crash through the airport fence. Eric Schulzinger's photograph shows the stricken 'Fort moments after the accident. The damage was serious and a volunteer CAF crew travelled to Burbank and spent several months putting the aircraft into ferriable condition for a flight back to Mesa, where further repairs were undertaken enabling the bomber to continue its airshow tours by spring of 1989

Above The Arizona Wing of the CAF has put a tremendous amount of money and effort into N9323Z to keep the vintage bomber flying. During 1962, Western Air became Aero Union at Chico, California, and the company became the largest American operator of civil 'Forts. The aircraft was painted in the distinctive house colours and in 1965 was fitted with Aero Union's streamlined fibreglass nose modification

Left As the gleaming skin of N9323Z testifies, the Arizona Wing of the CAF has put in countless hours keeping *Sentimental Journey* in fine shape. During its life with Aero Union, Tanker 17 transversed the country attacking fires. However, in 1977 the company took the bomber to the annual CAF airshow at Harlingen, Texas, in the hope of finding a buyer but there were no takers, even though the asking price was only in the vicinity of $50,000. Shortly afterwards, the CAF Arizona Wing pooled enough money and purchased the aircraft which was flown to their Mesa base

Above Over the years, virtually all of the original military equipment has been added to the B-17G, even down to the K6 gun mounts in the waist position. The Arizona Wing is diligent in tracking down any lead regarding original equipment for their aircraft, or for the other B-17s still flying

Left Betty Grable was one of World War 2's most popular pin-up girls and her graceful form adorns the nose of *Sentimental Journey*. All three power-turrets on the 'Fort work, which is something of a rarity on a restored B-17

Above A lurid California sunset outlines the distinctive profile of *Sentimenal Journey*. There are absolutely no plans to ground this vintage bomber, which is currently enjoying even more popularity since it is the 50th anniversary of World War 2

Left The bright blue markings of the 457th Bomb Group and polished metal skin of N9323Z have become a familiar sight at airshows across America. Now with an excess of over 7000 flying hours, the B-17G logs between 150/175 hours per year on its cross-country tours raising funds for the CAF and earning income to keep the aircraft operational

Miss Museum of Flying

Left The drama and magnificence of the Flying Fortress is amply illustrated in this banking shot. B-17G-105-VE USAAF s/n 44-85778 N3509G was delivered to the USAAF from Vega's Burbank factory on 6 June 1945, and, like the majority of other surviving 'Forts, immediately went to a modification centre (where the latest updates were added, rather than at the factory, which would have delayed production schedules) and then into storage at South Plains, Texas, on 9 September 1945

Below Fresh from a coat of paint at Aeroflair, Santa Maria, California, N3509G thunders east to Fort Lauderdale, Florida, on 10 June 1991 for in-depth restoration and addition of original military equipment for the October 1991 Museum of Flying Auction in Santa Monica, California. Once back on the West Coast, this vintage bomber was to be one of the top stars of the 70 classic aircraft put on the auction block. Going back several decades into its past though, the B-17 spent a few months in storage in Texas, before being returned to airworthy condition and flown to its first USAAF assignment with the Caribbean Air Command

Above With the four Wrights at full power, N3509G lifts off from Santa Maria for the flight to Florida with Don Whittington and Dick Churchill at the controls. While assigned to the Caribbean Air Command, '778 served with the 48th Search and Rescue Group and the 24th Composite Group. During early 1948, the aircraft was designated a TB-17G and by mid-year was transferred to Rio de Janeiro with the Brazilian Air Command, redesignated a VB-17G and used to transport members of the American embassy and staff officers

Right Although N3509G looks quite pristine in this view, the restoration job completed by World Jet (which was being finished as this book went to press) was superb. In late 1954, '778 travelled back to the 'States, this time to be based at Bolling AFB, Washington DC, where it was assigned to the 1100th Operational Group, probably once again hauling VIPs, until retirement and storage at Davis-Monthan AFB during 1956

Above Don Whittington and Dick Churchill hold the 'Fort steady as AT-6 camera-ship pilot Bruce Guberman comes in for some close formation flying. In 1959, '788 was put up for disposal along with most of the other surviving B-17s at Davis-Monthan, and the aircraft was purchased by Ace Smelting Company for $2888.88 on 14 August of that year. The price, by the way, was derived by taking the scrap value of aluminum per pound and multiplying that figure with the B-17's overall weight. Fortunately, the aircraft was not broken up but put up for sale

Right When purchased in a 1991 sheriff's sale, N3509G was missing a number of items including most of the engines. During 1990, Don Whittington had discovered an abandoned B-17E used in Boliva as a meat hauler and purchased the craft. After considerable work, Don got the aircraft airworthy and ferried it back to World Jet for complete restoration. After the purchase of '09G, Don sent a crew and the four engines to California to get it back into the air in record time

Left N3509G awaits its ferry flight to Florida. The Wright R-1820-97 radials produce 1200 horsepower each at 25,000 feet and are some of the most dependable aircraft engines ever built. In late 1960, Ace Smelting found a buyer for '09G and sold the aircraft to Sonora Flying Services in California, who intended to convert it into a fire bomber, but went out of business before the work could be undertaken

Above The Wrights on '09G had flown quite a few miles whilst fitted to the aircraft, but newly overhauled engines were installed during the Florida restoration. When Sonora Flying Services went out of business, a new buyer named Leo Demers stepped forward. In 1961, Demers flew the plane to his Madras, Oregon, base and converted the '09G to handle both the fire bombing and insect spraying missions. Operating as Tanker 97, Demers flew the aircraft for four years before putting it up for sale

Surrounded by light aircraft and looking not unlike some prehistoric beast, '09G sits on the Santa Maria ramp after getting its Aeroflair paint trim. Tanker 97 was purchased from Demers by Aero Union in Chico, California. Aero Union is one of the more professional air attack operators and they went through the 'Fort, removing the spraying capability and giving the aircraft the new identity of Tanker 16

Prior to launching from Santa Maria, Don Whittington thoroughly checked out the Wrights before the long trip across the 'States. The replacement engines never missed a beat during the ferry flight and the harshest task encountered was replenishing the oil in the engines, which involved climbing up on the wing and pouring quart bottles into the thirsty engines—American airfields are, unfortunately, no longer set up to handle the demands of large multi-piston engined aircraft

Above left Laura Wineman of Aeroflair applies the *Miss Museum of Flying* name to the polished forward fuselage of the 'Fort. The classic pin-up girl artwork was taken directly from the master of the female form, Alberto Vargas, whose artwork, albeit indirectly from the brush of the master, decorated thousands of American combat aircraft during World War 2. The computer-generated graphic was initiated by Chuck Smith at the museum, and then finished by Avilia Graphics for the final application to the nose of the bomber

Above right Don Whittington finishes checking the oil on one of the Wrights before the flight to Florida. Constantly in motion, Whittington functions as pilot and mechanic, transversing between such unusual aircraft as the B-17, his Griffon-powered P-51 racer, and his newly-restored Grumman F9F-8T Cougar without the slightest problem

Right When Whittington picked up the bomber at Stockton, California, after his restoration team had brought the old bird back to life, a new nose piece had been fitted along with a replica chin turret (note the authentic canvas zipper slots for the twin .50 calibre Brownings). Chin turrets are virtually impossible to find, although we are sure that somewhere in America there is a forgotten warehouse with turrets packed away in dusty crates!

Left During its life with Aero Union, the company fitted '09G with a new streamlined fibreglass nose. This was done for a couple of reasons. Firstly, the old plexiglass units were tending to explode in flight and, secondly, the new units actually added a vital few mph to the 'Fort's top speed. Aero Union operated the B-17 from 1966 to 1972, when it was sold to Central Air Services of Wenatchee, Washington, who operated it as Tanker 42. The new nose was added in June 1968. The aircraft is seen between fires at Omak, Washington, during August 1973

Above Seen in its distinctive Aero Union scheme, Tanker 16 awaits the fortunes of nature on 24 April 1968 at Wilmington, North Carolina, still with its original nose piece. Dempsey sold '09G to Western Aviation Contractors in 1978, and they operated it for three years from American Fork, Utah, as Tanker 102 until selling the 'Fort to a broker, who in turn sold the aircraft in 1982 to Aircraft Component Equipment Supplies. The B-17 then sat at Mojave Airport in California for a bit, before moving to Stockton, California, to spend nearly a decade in storage, culminating in a 1991 sheriff's sale

Nine-O-Nine

Left With its Wrights beating out a thunderous note of defiant survival, B-17G-85-DL USAAF s/n 44-83575 N93012 breaks away from the Twin Beech camera-ship on 16 August 1991 over Geneseo, New York. Originally delivered from the Douglas, Long Beach, California, factory on 7 April 1945 to the USAAF, this aircraft has one of the strangest records of survival of any Flying Fortress

Below The annual gathering of Flying Fortresses at Geneseo '91 welcomed back into the fold N93012, which was flown in spirited style by Gary Young for our photo mission. Following delivery to the USAAF, this B-17 was flown to a mod centre at Tulsa, Oklahoma, and then on to another mod centre at Cheyenne, Wyoming (where the Cheyenne tail turret picked up its name), before being readied for service during May 1945. After this point, the service history of the aircraft is very shadowy

Left *Nine-o-Nine*, in flight during August 1991, displays its fairly accurate markings (although the rendition of faded olive drab is a bit curious—the nose markings were originally applied by Tony Starcer, who is mentioned in the *Memphis Belle* chapter). This aircraft was assigned to the Caribbean Air Command (6th Air Force) during 1947 and was apparently modified to TB-17H configuration, indicating an air–sea rescue mission with the large Higgins A1 lifeboat slung under the fuselage, along with other associated modifications. Assigned to the 1st Rescue Squadron, the aircraft spent time at several bases in the Caribbean during its tour of duty

Above The Collings Foundation, current owners of the 'Fort, campaign the rare warbird around the country as part of their educational and fund raising programme. John Rising is seen performing some work on a propeller hub between airshow routines. When the air–sea mission for the B-17 was deemed finished, the aircraft was flown to Yucca Flats, Mercury (an appropriately named hell-hole), Nevada, to be staked out for atomic blast testing to determine what damage would be done to airframes by an above surface explosion. This was at a time when the government apparently believed that the health of the general population would not be affected by above ground explosions (hopefully, the prevailing winds were dumping lots of radioactivity on the politicos in 'DC). The B-17s were flown in and then towed to the site by unfortunate individuals (who we are almost certain no longer shuffle this mortal coil), and then strategically placed at differing locations from bomb blasts to determine the effects

Below With the suitably bureaucratic title of 'Vulnerability of Parked Aircraft to Atomic Bombs', '575 was subjected to above-ground atomic bomb detonations, being placed at various distances from ground zero. The first test saw '575 parked a mere 10,000 feet from the explosion (one kiloton). In the second, a 31 kiloton bomb was set off at the same distance and this time '575 was damaged—which the testing organization determined would take 4000 hours to fix. The third test saw the bomber moved to within 8000 ft of a 19 kiloton blast, doing a further 5274 repair hours of damage. A total of 28 aircraft were used in the test, the conclusion of which stated that tail draggers with large wing areas were most likely to be damaged. Brilliant! It was determined that the aircraft were sufficiently 'cool' in 1964 to sell for scrap. Aero Specialities purchased the B-17, rebuilt it on the desert floor, and flew it to Mesa, Arizona, for a twelve-year rebuild. Seen during 1969, a great deal of the sheet metal has been replaced but the USAF MATS markings are still clearly visible

Right By 1977, Tanker 99 was ready to join the Aircraft Specialities fleet. Since they had plenty of time, the company rebuilt the 'Fort to the exact configuration they wanted, removing virtually every bit of military equipment in the process. Rigged for spraying and retardant dropping, the aircraft was a faithful worker until auctioned off in October 1985 to Bob Collings, who sent it to Tom Reilly's 'Bombertown' in Florida for a complete rebuild back to military specs, N93012 emerging as *Nine-o-Nine*. However, a pilot induced accident at Beaver County Airport, Pennsylvania, on 23 August 1987 saw the bomber nearly written off. Several years of hard work by volunteers got the B-17 back into ferriable condition, and it went to Reilly's for another rebuild to emerge in the pristine condition seen on these pages

Texas Raiders

Left With its great nose art and flags waving, *Texas Raiders* is a star attraction at any airshow. B-17G-95-DL USAAF s/n 44-83872 N7227C was the first Flying Fortress acquired by the Confederate Air Force. On 12 July 1945, the USAAF accepted the aircraft from the Douglas factory, but the aircraft was immediately transferred to the US Navy for PB-1W conversion. Flown to NAS Johnsville, Pennsylvania, suitable modifications were undertaken to convert the 'Fort to the Navy mission. Assigned Bureau Number 77235, the PB-1W was not given an operational mission until mid-1947, when it was delivered to NAS Quonset Point and VX-4

Below An evening sun over Geneseo on 16 August 1991, highlights the distinctive features of *Texas Raiders*. BuNo 77235 flew with VX-4 and VW-2 for nearly seven years and carried out a number of experiments for the Naval Aircraft Development Center. During 1954, the PB-1W flew to Japan to join VW-1, an early warning squadron, at Atsugi. The aircraft barely remained a year at this assignment before being withdrawn from service and flown to Litchfield Park, Arizona—the Navy's equivalent of Davis-Monthan—on 15 January 1955 for storage and disposal

Texas Raiders is seen during July 1988 near Camarillo, California, on one of its regular swings across the United States in support of the CAF. The B-17 was put up for sale in 1957 and purchased by Aero Service Corporation in Philadelphia for $17,510. Aero Service operated a diverse selection of aircraft in the mapping role. This aircraft being suitably modified to perform this task as N7227C. Lots of money was lavished on the aircraft and a large cargo door was installed on the left side of the fuselage, the B-17 travelling the globe in its new mission

Above This close-up view of *Texas Raiders* on 13 November 1990, shows the huge amount of work that has gone into N7227C. Over the years, the CAF began to make progress with the aircraft, adding turrets and getting rid of the cargo door. In 1983, the 'Fort was pulled from service and the CAF's Gulf Coast Wing took over responsibility for the old warrior, affecting a complete rebuild. Once work on the airframe had been finished, the B-17 was resprayed as a wartime aircraft from the 533rd Bomb Squadron/381st Bomb Group. As can be clearly seen, the resulting aircraft was a stunning tribute to the dedication of the Gulf Coast Wing

Left and overleaf Above a California fog deck, a fully-restored *Texas Raiders* displays its impressive array of original military equipment. The aircraft performed faithfully for Aero Service, but as it grew older and parts became harder to find, N7227C was sold to the CAF on 22 September 1967 for the then not inconsiderable sum of $50,000. Painted in civil colours, the CAF added a Confederate flag and little else. During this early time period, the CAF obtained the reputation of operating a poorly maintained fleet of former military aircraft in a variety of incorrect markings, and crashes were not uncommon. As the years went on, N727C began to look a little ratty. However, as the worldwide preservation trend grew, the aircraft took on a rough military paint scheme in 1970, with markings from the 305th Bomb Group

Above Photographed in October 1976 at Harlingen, Texas, N7227C displays the first military style scheme it wore in CAF service. At this time, no turrets were fitted and the large cargo door was still in place

Left Work on the veteran bomber is on-going at the craft's Houston base, and a coffee can is seen being temporarily affixed to contain an oil leak. Along with sister-ship *Sentimental Journey*, *Texas Raiders* is regularly flown across the country to raise funds to support its operation

Thunderbird

Right Seen on 13 November 1990 while on final approach prior to arrival at its new home of Galveston, Texas, is B-17G-105-VE USAAF s/n 44-85718 N900RW. The aircraft was being ferried, gear down, from its former home at Houston-Hobby Airport to the magnificent new Lone Star Flight Museum at Galveston. This particular aircraft is one of the hundreds of new 'Forts that went immediately into storage before being put up for sale by the Reconstruction Finance Corporation (RFC)

Below A great deal of restoration work had taken place by the time of our photo flight on 13 November 1990, but more work still needed to be done and the ever-vigilant museum director, Jim Fausz elected to make the ferry flight gear down. The hop was short and successful and, since these photos were taken, N900RW has been the subject of much more work to bring the aircraft up to the museum's exacting standards. Unfortunately, a planned flight from Oakland to Pearl Harbor on 7 December 1991 fell through because of the lack of a suitable sponsor. Through a broker, IGN purchased four Altus 'Forts during 1947, '718 being one of the lucky aircraft to escape scrapping. Strangely, all aircraft were sold with full military equipment (except for the .50 calibre Brownings) and '718 received the French registration F-BEEC for the flight from Oklahoma to Creil, France

N900RW's shadow chases the bomber as pilots Ronnie Gardner and Jim Fausz prepare to touch down at Galveston. B-17G '718 was extremely lucky since most of its stablemates were chopped up to be fed into aluminum ingot furnaces. Immediately after the war, France's *Institut Geographique National* (IGN) began acquiring B-17s as a perfect high-altitude platform for the company's worldwide mapping and survey operations, scouts from IGN checking out the vast RFC airfields across the country. Delivered from Vega on 8 May 1945, '718 was an ideal candidate since its only flying time was between the factory and storage facilities. The final resting place for the virtually new 'Fort was Altus, Oklahoma, where it was surrounded by hundreds of other warplanes on its 21 November 1945 arrival

Right With its new home immediately in the background, N900RW sets up for its first landing at Galveston. Two huge world-class hangars have been constructed to house the growing Lone Star collection, which comprises both flying aircraft and airframes under restoration to flying condition. After more than three decades of service with the IGN, F-BEEC was sold to Doug Arnold in Britain as G-FORT, before being sold once again to Lone Star on 9 June 1987

Below Whilst Lone Star mechanics swarmed over the 'Fort in Britain, getting the aircraft ready for its long flight to Texas, it was decided to paint the bomber as *Thunderbird* of the 303rd Bomb Group. An original crewman was even found who was willing to make the transatlantic flight, and with a great deal of fanfare, the B-17 left the Imperial War Museum field at Duxford on 14 July 1987 for the successful flight back to America

Left The colourful red markings of the 303rd BG stand out dramatically against N900RW's camouflage. As can be seen, Fausz's dedicated crew have added a completely rebuilt original tail gun position, along with numerous original interior fittings. The aircraft had been stripped while in IGN service and finding the original hardware has proven time-consuming and difficult. The entire airframe has been inspected for corrosion and physical defects, all of which have been repaired to the highest standards where necessary

Below This close-in view of N900RW just after its arrival at Galveston shows many of the modifications carried out by the IGN for their mapping and survey flights. Lone Star has now removed all these non-standard items and returned the aircraft to its original wartime configuration. The bomber toured the airshow circuit in 1991, along with many of the other airworthy warbirds flown by Lone Star

Above As a closing view, we see F-BEEC in impeccable but drab IGN markings in France during the 1970s. Thanks to the IGN, several of today's 'Forts are still capable of flight. The company operated at least 14 B-17Gs for over three decades

Chuckie

Right Its broad bare metal wings covering a chunk of west Texas landscape, B-17G-70-VE USAAF s/n 44-8543 N3710G heads in for a landing at Breckenridge, Texas, during May 1986. The early military records of this 'Fort do not exist, but the aircraft was delivered from the Vega factory on 17 October 1944 to the USAAF. It is thought, but currently not proven, that the B-17 may have travelled to Europe for combat and it does appear that some repairs to the bomber's belly may have been affected following battle damage

Below Seen once again on approach to Howard Pardue's annual warbird show at Breckenridge, Texas (one of the world's best warbird events), *Chuckie* shows a number of improvements during May 1987, including a highly-polished aluminum skin. The first available records for the bomber begin in late 1945, when the aircraft was being utilized as a TB-17G trainer at Patterson Field, Ohio. The aircraft then participated in a number of other assignments, including serving with the All Weather Flying Center, and several photos exist of the B-17 modified (designated ETB-17G) to test a variety of electronic equipment

Above While heading for Breckenridge during May 1987, we ran into one of the typical summer downpours that happen very suddenly. It is safest to stay locked into formation and the resulting photo is a somewhat unusual spectacle of the 'Fort droning through a shower. During its recorded military life, the bomber was transferred to different test assignments and was assigned to the Federal Telecommunication Corporation in New York and New Jersey to test various electronic equipment installations. The aircraft was retired in March 1959 and flown to Davis-Monthan AFB for disposal

Right Currently owned by Doc Hospers and named for his wife Chuckie (who is one of the sparkplugs of the B-17 Co-op), N3701G is based at historic Meacham Field, Fort Worth, Texas. When N3701G was surplused, it was purchased by American Compressed Steel/Aero-American Corporation and flown to Texas, where a cargo door was installed. During early 1961, the B-17 was sold to a company that hauled fruits and vegetables but this, needless to say, did not last long and, in 1963, N3701G went to Dothan Aviation in Alabama where it was modified as a bug sprayer. When environmentalist laws took over in 1976, Dothan's 'Forts were withdrawn from the deadly spraying role and the B-17s (N3701G and N5017N) were both in very poor condition. N3701G was sold to Dr William Hospers on 4 October 1979, and since then Doc, Chuckie, and a dedicated crew of volunteers have slowly worked to bring the 'Fort back to its original wartime configuration. Painted in the markings of the 486th Bomb Group, *Chuckie* regularly attends airshows across the 'States

Sally B

Left Without a doubt, *Sally B* is the most famous European Flying Fortress. B-17G-105-VE USAAF s/n 44-85784 G-BEDF was delivered to the USAAF from Vega at Burbank on 19 June 1945. Going into storage, the aircraft was eventually assigned a testing role as an EB-17G, and then redesigned an ETB-17G in April 1949

Below This detail view shows the fine condition of *Sally B* during June 1986. The aircraft retained its 457th BG markings until July 1989 when it was suitably modified as a B-17F for the film *Memphis Belle*, a role which added a needed infusion of operating cash. Since then, the aircraft has been even more popular on the European airshow circuit

Left United Kingdom airpower at its best. In this June 1986 view, Chris Bevans pilots the 'Fort while being escorted by Stephen Grey in his P-51D and Steve Hinton in Grey's P-47D Thunderbolt on a misty day near the Duxford home base for all three aircraft. Soon after being declared surplus, the B-17G was sold to the *Institut Geographique National* in France as F-BGSR. As with other B-17s purchased by the French concern, the aircraft was configured to the survey/mapping role. The aircraft was withdrawn from service in 1970 and purchased by Ted White and Duane Egli as N17TE. The B-17 soon became a popular airshow attraction. White was killed in a T-6 crash and, reportedly, Egli was hung while serving as a mercenary during an African insurrection. Under the dynamic guidance of Sally Ellingboe and the B-17 Preservation Ltd, the 'Fort has prospered at its Duxford home base. Painted in the markings of the 457th Bomb Group, the 'Fort is one of Europe's most prized airshow attractions

Above Out to pasture at Creil. This August 1967 view of F-BGSR shows that the grass has not been mowed under the aircraft for some time—indicative of an extreme lack of movement. It is quite amazing that IGN kept its 'Forts going for such a long period, and it is to the credit of this company that several of today's 'Forts are still airworthy

Aluminium Overcast

Left With tail wheel fixed firmly down, B-17G-105-VE USAAF s/n 44-85740 N5017N is seen orbiting near Titusville, Florida, during March 1983 at the annual Valiant Air Command warbird airshow. Built by Lockheed's Vega division at Burbank, California, and delivered to the USAAF on 17 May 1945, the aircraft joined hundreds of other new 'Forts in storage, the Air Force simply having no use for the aircraft at this late stage of the war. Stored at Syracuse, New York, the bomber was declared surplus for military use and flown to Altus, Oklahoma, on 7 November 1945. Altus was one of several fields around the country that either sold aircraft to civilian pilots or scrappers—unfortunately the scrappers were usually in the majority

Below This close-in view shows the complete lack of military equipment on *Aluminum Overcast*, while the odd fairing under the nose is probably a left-over from its civilian aerial survey days. Once at Altus, the aircraft sat for 18 months before purchased for $750 by a company called Metal Products, probably for scrap. However, the aircraft was turned around in one month and sold to Universal Aviation for $1800—a handsome return on investment. Sold once again to an outfit called Vero Beach Import and Export Company, the 'Fort was modified as a cargo hauler and began flying cattle between Florida and Puerto Rico during 1947, having only flown a total of 37 flying hours up to this point! Based in Philadelphia, Aero Service was a large survey and mapping company that operated a number of ex-military aircraft, purchasing N5017N in mid-1949 for a whopping $28,000. Modified for high-altitude mapping, the aircraft was completely disassembled and rebuilt by Aero Services, before commencing operations travelling the world on its new assignment, logging well over 3000 hours in just three years

A rather bedraggled N5017N in storage during June 1964 after purchase by Stolzfus and Associates of Coatsville, Pennsylvania. The company intended to convert the 'Fort into a sprayer, but this never happened and the bomber was sold to Dothan Aviation in Alabama during 1966 for fire ant spraying, being suitably modified soon after arrival in the southern state. Accumulating many more flying hours, the B-17 was eventually pensioned off in 1976 when the government sponsored programme ended. In 1978, the 'Fort was sold to well-known warbird collector Dr Bill Harrison, who spent time and money bringing the aircraft back to flying status for a proposed around-the-world goodwill flight, but this unfortunately fell through and N5017N was generously donated to the Experimental Aircraft Association for display at its Oshkosh museum. Since then, the flying hours of *Aluminum Overcast* have been severely restricted, but some military equipment has been added, although a less than authentic off-grey paint job has detracted from its original military appearance